PRESC

MW00681516

To _____

From _____

1

PRESCRIPTION

Prescription for Life
Copyright © 1997 by The Zondervan Corporation
ISBN 0-310-97375-9

Requests for information should be addressed to:

ZondervanPublishingHouse
Mail Drop B20
Grand Rapids, Michigan 49530
http://www.zondervan.com

Senior Editor: Joy Marple
Project Editor: Joe Lacy
Production Editor: Pat Matuszak
Creative Manager: Patricia Matthews
Design: Mark Veldheer

Printed in The United States of America
97 98 99/DP/ 3 2

PRESCRIPTION

Teach us to number our days aright, that we may gain a heart of wisdom.

Psalm 90:12

PRESCRIPTION

Your lifestyle can affect your longevity. Here are some lifestyle habits that are associated with long life:

Engage in routines requiring activity.

Accept challenges and don't allow life to become too easy. If you're in above your head, recognize it and seek an alternative.

Keep a relaxed attitude.

Flexibility. Includes physical and psychological ability to bend, not break.

JA Lacy and R Lacy

PRESCRIPTION

Blessed is the man who finds wisdom,
   the man who gains understanding,
For she is more profitable than silver
   and yields better returns than gold.
She is more precious than rubies;
   nothing you desire can compare with her.
Long life is in her right hand;
   in her left hand are riches and honor.
Her ways are pleasant ways,
   and all her paths are peace.

Proverbs 3:13-17

PRESCRIPTION

Good character is more to be praised than outstanding talent. Most talents are, to some extent, a gift. Good character, by contrast, is not given to us. We have to build it piece by piece—by thought, choice, courage, and determination.

J Luther

6

PRESCRIPTION

Whatever you do, work at it with
all your heart, as working for the Lord, not
for men, since you know that you will receive
an inheritance from the Lord as a reward. It
is the Lord Christ you are serving.

Colossians 3:23,24

PRESCRIPTION

Die when I may, I want it said of me
by those who knew me best, that I always
plucked a thistle and planted a flower where
I thought a flower would grow.

A Lincoln

PRESCRIPTION

We should all be concerned about
the future because we will have to spend
the rest of our lives there.

Kettering

PRESCRIPTION

One of the greatest benefits to be gleaned from
the Bible is perspective. When we get discouraged,
we temporarily lose our perspective. Focusing on
God's word for even ten or fifteen minutes allows
you to put daily issues into perspective.

JA Lacy

PRESCRIPTION

Let us not love with words or tongue
but with actions and in truth.

1 John 3:18

PRESCRIPTION

It is a curious fact that when you get sick you want an uncommon doctor; if your car breaks down, you want an uncommonly good mechanic; when we get into war we dreadfully want an uncommon admiral or an uncommon general. I have never met a father and mother who did not want their children to grow up to be uncommon men and women. May it always be so. For the future of America rests not in mediocrity, but in the constant renewal of leadership in every phase of our national life.

H Hoover

PRESCRIPTION

Delight yourself in the LORD and he will
give you the desires of your heart.

Psalm 37:4

PRESCRIPTION

Only God who can see the invisible
can do the impossible.

Author unknown

PRESCRIPTION

To him who is able to keep you from falling
  and to present you before his glorious presence
  without fault and with great joy—
To the only God our Savior be glory, majesty,
  power and authority,
Through Jesus Christ our Lord, before all ages,
  now and forevermore! Amen.

Jude 1:24-25

PRESCRIPTION

Not only so, but we also rejoice in our sufferings, because we know that suffering produces perseverance; perseverance, character; and character, hope. And hope does not disappoint us, because God has poured out his love into our hearts by the Holy Spirit, whom he has given us.

Romans 5:3-5

PRESCRIPTION

Jesus grew in wisdom and stature, and in favor with God and men (Luke 2:52). Jesus grew mentally, physically, spiritually and socially. What a powerful example of a life fully lived!

JA Lacy

PRESCRIPTION

The secret of your own heart you
can never know; but you can know him
who knows its secret.

G MacDonald

PRESCRIPTION

The LORD bless you and keep you;
The LORD make his face shine
  upon you and be gracious to you;
The LORD turn his face toward you
  and give you peace.

Numbers 6:24-26

19

℞ PRESCRIPTION

Life is no brief candle to me. It is a sort of splendid torch which I have got hold of for the moment, and I want to make it burn as brightly as possible before handing it to future generations.

GB Shaw

PRESCRIPTION

Give, and it will be given to you. A good measure, pressed down, shaken together and running over, will be poured into your lap. For with the measure you use, it will be measured to you.

Luke 6:38

PRESCRIPTION

Heed how thou livest. Do no act by day which
from the night shall drive thy peace away.

Whittier

22

PRESCRIPTION

The wisdom that comes from heaven is first of all pure; then peace-loving, considerate, submissive, full of mercy and good fruit, impartial and sincere. Peacemakers who sow in peace raise a harvest of righteousness.

James 3:17-18

PRESCRIPTION

Perseverance is not a long race;
it is many short races one after another.

W Elliott

24

PRESCRIPTION

Be joyful always; pray continually; give
thanks in all circumstances, for this is
God's will for you in Christ Jesus.

1 Thessalonians 5:16-18

PRESCRIPTION

Lord, help me to capture the day;
  enlighten me with the wisdom of Your vision.
Let me take the day's problems
  and work them with hand and mind
so that the product is a glory to You and a peace
  to me.

JA Lacy

PRESCRIPTION

The LORD is my shepherd,
I shall not be in want.

Psalm 23:1

PRESCRIPTION

We are never more like Jesus than
when we are selflessly, lovingly, reaching
out to meet somebody else's needs.

Author uknown

PRESCRIPTION

Long life to you! Good health to you
and your household! And good health
to all that is yours!

1 Samuel 25:6

PRESCRIPTION

We know life's never measured
by how many years we live,
But by the kindly things we do
and the happiness we give.

HS Rice

PRESCRIPTION

"For I know the plans I have for you,"
declares the LORD, "plans to prosper you
and not to harm you, plans to give you
hope and a future."

Jeremiah 29:11

RPRESCRIPTION

Look at a day when you are supremely satisfied
at the end. It's not a day when you lounge
around doing nothing; it's when you've had
everything to do, and you've done it.

M Thatcher

PRESCRIPTION

Smile at people. It takes 72 muscles to frown and only 14 to smile.

Author Unknown

PRESCRIPTION

The fear of the LORD is the beginning
of knowledge.

Proverbs 1:7

PRESCRIPTION

In the morning, O Lord,
   you hear my voice;
in the morning I lay my requests before
   you and wait in expectation.

Psalm 5:3

PRESCRIPTION

A good character is the best tombstone. Those who loved you and were helped by you will remember you when forget-me-nots have withered. Carve your name on hearts, not on marble.

CH Spurgeon

PRESCRIPTION

The LORD does not look at the things man looks at. Man looks at the outward appearance, but the LORD looks at the heart.

1 Samuel 16:7

PRESCRIPTION

Balance and moderation are two keys to successful living. Overworking is any situation where a person is spending hours on his or her vocation to the exclusion of other priority areas, such as family, church, and personal time.

R Crosson

PRESCRIPTION

Come to me [Jesus], all you who are weary
and burdened, and I will give you rest.

Matthew 11:28

PRESCRIPTION

Be alert to give service. What counts a great deal in life is what we do for others.

Author unknown

PRESCRIPTION

For God so loved the world that he gave his one and only Son, that whoever believes in him shall not perish but have eternal life.

John 3:16

PRESCRIPTION

That best little portion of a good man's life—
his little, nameless, unremembered acts
of kindness and love.

W Wordsworth

PRESCRIPTION

The happiness of life is made up of minute fractions-the little soon forgotten charities of a kiss or smile, a kind look, a heartfelt compliment, and the countless infinitesimals of pleasurable and genial feeling.

W Scott

PRESCRIPTION

The fear of the LORD adds length to life.

Proverbs 10:27

44

PRESCRIPTION

I shall pass through this world but once.
Any good that I can do,
   or any kindness that I can show any human
   being, let me do it now and not defer it.
For I shall not pass this way again.

W Penn

PRESCRIPTION

I will never forget your precepts, for by
them you have preserved my life.

Psalm 119:93

PRESCRIPTION

Whether we live 10 years or 100 years, in the scheme of things, eternity is only a moment away. Eternity is always perched on our doorstep. Life is a limited, fragile currency of time. Exchange yours for what you deem most important.

JA Lacy

PRESCRIPTION

All Scripture is God-breathed and
is useful for teaching, rebuking, correcting
and training in righteousness.

2 Timothy 3:16

PRESCRIPTION

Walking uplifts the spirit. Breathe out the poisons of tension, stress, and worry; breathe in the power of God. Send forth little silent prayers of goodwill towards those you meet. Walk with a sense of being a part of a vast universe. Consider the thousands of miles of earth beneath your feet; think of the limitless expanse of space above your head. Walk in awe, wonder, and humility.

W Peterson

PRESCRIPTION

Religious activity, Bible study, our personal devotions must be a preparation, not a substitution, for dealing with pivotal choices facing all of us: What am I giving my life to? Do my goals, ambitions, and values reflect the beliefs I espouse? How much of what I consider important does God consider valuable in light of eternity?

Rinehart

PRESCRIPTION

The LORD is my strength and my shield;
my heart trusts in him, and I am helped.
My heart leaps for joy and I will give
thanks to him in song.

Psalm 28:7

51

PRESCRIPTION

When you need to change something in your life, think about these questions:

What are the barriers to change?

What do I gain with change?

How can I facilitate change?

By what date do I want change to occur?

If you know your own goals,

you'll be amazed at the opportunities you will have to accomplish them.

Author unknown

PRESCRIPTION

Keep my commands and you will live;
guard my teachings as the apple
of your eye.

Proverbs 7:2

PRESCRIPTION

Thought is supreme. Preserve a mental attitude—the attitude of courage, frankness, and good cheer. To think rightly is to create. All things come through desire and every sincere prayer is answered. We become like that on which our thoughts are fixed.

E Hubbard

PRESCRIPTION

Finally, brothers, whatever is true,
whatever is noble, whatever is right, whatever
is pure, whatever is lovely, whatever is
admirable—if anything is excellent or
praiseworthy—think about such things.

Philippians 4:8

PRESCRIPTION

To live contentedly with small means; to seek elegance rather than luxury, and refinement rather than fashion; to be worthy, not respectable, and wealthy, not rich; to study hard, think quietly, talk gently, act frankly; to listen to stars and birds, to babes and sages, with open heart; to bear all cheerfully, do all bravely, await occasions, hurry never. In a word, to let the spiritual, unbidden and unconscious, grow up through the common. This is to be my symphony.

Channing

PRESCRIPTION

The Bible, the greatest medicine
chest of humanity.

H Heine

PRESCRIPTION

God loves each one of us, as if there were only one of us.

St Augustine

58

PRESCRIPTION

Maintaining proper perspective
on emotions is a powerful key to health
and strength.

J Schindler

PRESCRIPTION

Just as it is good for a person to know that of himself he can do nothing, it is also good for him to know that he can do all things with God.

Author Unknown

PRESCRIPTION

The LORD loves righteousness and justice; the earth is full of his unfailing love. By the word of the LORD were the heavens made, their starry host by the breath of his mouth.

Psalm 33:5-6

PRESCRIPTION

Discipline is the refining fire by which
talent becomes ability.

Smith

PRESCRIPTION

Therefore, if anyone is in Christ,
he is a new creation; the old has gone,
the new has come!

2 Corinthians 5:17

PRESCRIPTION

When love and skill work together,
expect a masterpiece.

Ruskin

64

PRESCRIPTION

A heart at peace gives life to the body.

Proverbs 14:30

PRESCRIPTION

Be generous and understanding. Let no one
come to you without feeling better and happier
when they leave. Be the living expression of God's
kindness: with kindness on your face, kindness
in your eyes, kindness in your smile, kindness
in your warm greeting.

Mother Teresa

℞ PRESCRIPTION

The LORD is my shepherd, I shall not be in want.
He makes me lie down in green pastures,
He leads me beside quiet waters,
He restores my soul.
He guides me in paths of righteousness
  for his name's sake.

Psalm 23:1-3

PRESCRIPTION

Body Building

We build up the body with nutrition and exercise,
but how do we build up the body of Christ?
Through fellowship, training and service in love.

A Aronis

PRESCRIPTION

Man was made for his God,
and he is completely out of sorts until
he has found him.

E Fesche

PRESCRIPTION

Wisdom is supreme; therefore
get wisdom. Though it cost all you have,
get understanding.

Proverbs 4:7

PRESCRIPTION

Setting Goals

One way people try to achieve things in life is to set goals. Examine your life to see that your goals line up with the Lord's will for your life.

JA Lacy

PRESCRIPTION

I am the light of the world. Whoever
follows me will never walk in darkness,
but will have the light of life.

John 8:12

PRESCRIPTION

Love is the greatest thing that God can give us;
for he himself is love: and it is the greatest thing
we can give to God; for it will also give ourselves,
and carry with it all that is ours.

Taylor

PRESCRIPTION

I can do everything through him
who gives me strength.

Philippians 4:13

PRESCRIPTION

Wesley's Rule:
Do all the good you can,
By all the means you can,
In all the ways you can,
In all the places you can,
At all the times you can,
To all the people you can,
As long as you ever can.

Edwards

PRESCRIPTION

I never did anything worth doing by accident, nor did any of my inventions come by accidents; they came by work.

T Edison

PRESCRIPTION

Do not be wise in your own eyes;
fear the LORD and shun evil. This will bring
health to your body and nourishment
to your bones.

Proverbs 3:7-8

PRESCRIPTION

Take time to work—it is the price of success.
Take time to think—it is the source of power.
Take time to play—it is the secret of perpetual youth.
Take time to read—it is the fountain of wisdom.
Take time to be friendly—it is the road to happiness.
Take time to dream—it is hitching your wagon to a star.
Take time to love and be loved—it is the example of God.
Take time to look around—the day is too short to be
   selfish.
Take time to laugh—it is the music of the soul.

Old Irish Prayer

PRESCRIPTION

No eye has seen, no ear has heard,
no mind has conceived what God has
prepared for those who love him.

1 Corinthians 2:9

R℞ PRESCRIPTION

A man suffering from insomnia asked
a friend how he managed to get to sleep so easily
each night. "Do you count sheep?"

"No," he replied, "I talk to the Shepherd."

H Taylor

PRESCRIPTION

Trust in the LORD and do good.

Psalm 37:3

PRESCRIPTION

The life that intends to be wholly obedient, wholly submissive, wholly listening, is astonishing in its completeness. Its joys are ravishing, its peace profound, its humility the deepest, its power world shaking, its love enveloping, its simplicity that of a trusting child.

Kelly

PRESCRIPTION

But when you pray, go into your room, close
the door and pray to your Father, who is unseen.
Then your Father, who sees what is done in
secret, will reward you.

Matthew 6:6

PRESCRIPTION

There is only one basis for really enjoying life, and that is to walk in the way in which God leads you.

Author Unknown

PRESCRIPTION

The joy of the LORD is your strength.

Nehemiah 8:10

85

PRESCRIPTION

The joy of the LORD is your strength.

Nehemiah 8:10

PRESCRIPTION

Great works are performed not by strength,
but by perseverance.

Johnson

PRESCRIPTION

There is no power on earth that can neutralize the influence of a high, pure, simple, and useful life.

BT Washington

PRESCRIPTION

Be strong in the Lord and
in his mighty power.

Ephesians 6:10

PRESCRIPTION

The body is made to move. Regular activity results in: healthy muscle tone, a strong heart, improved circulation, endurance, and strong body supporting structures. ("Do you not know that your body is a temple of the Holy Spirit, who is in you, whom you have received from God? You are not your own; you were bought at a price. Therefore honor God with your body." 1Corinthians 6:19-20)

JA Lacy and R Lacy

PRESCRIPTION

Pay attention and listen to the sayings of the wise; apply your heart to what I teach, for it is pleasing when you keep them in your heart and have all of them ready on your lips.

Proverbs 22:17-18

PRESCRIPTION

Genius develops in quiet places,
character out in the full current
of human life.

Goethe

PRESCRIPTION

Commit your way to the LORD; trust in him and he will do this: He will make your righteousness shine like the dawn, the justice of your cause like the noonday sun.

Psalm 37:5-6

PRESCRIPTION

Jesus came in peace to a world of strife. He came in hope to a world of despair. He came with light to a world of darkness. He came with life for you and me.

C Grant

93

PRESCRIPTION

God asks no man whether he will
accept life. That is not his choice. You must
take it. The only choice is how.

HW Beecher

PRESCRIPTION

I have come that they may have life,
and have it to the full.

John 10:10

PRESCRIPTION

If you can't fly, run. If you can't run, walk. If you can't walk, crawl. But by all means, keep moving.

ML King

PRESCRIPTION

Above all else, guard your heart,
for it is the wellspring of life.

Proverbs 4:23

PRESCRIPTION

Diet Impacts Health

Roughly 98% of people born in the US are healthy. Then we spend the rest of our lives accumulating risk factors. How we eat impacts almost half of the ten leading causes of death—atherosclerosis, cancer, diabetes, and heart disease. A major concern is not nutrient deficiency, but excess and imbalance of dietary components.

JA Lacy

PRESCRIPTION

Fear God and keep his commandments,
for this is the whole duty of man.

Ecclesiastes 12:13

PRESCRIPTION

From one day to another
God will gladly give
To everyone who seeks him
and tries each day to live
A little bit more closely
to God and to each other.

HS Rice

PRESCRIPTION

Great peace have they who love God's law,
and nothing can make them stumble.

Psalm 119:165

PRESCRIPTION

All men must work, but no man should work
beyond his physical and intellectual ability,
nor beyond the hours which nature allots.
No net result of good to the individual nor the
race comes of any artificial prolonging of the
day at either end. Work while it is day.
When night comes, rest.

C Spurgeon

PRESCRIPTION

And God blessed the seventh day and made it holy, because on it he rested from all the work of creating that he had done.

Genesis 2:3

103

PRESCRIPTION

Far better it is to dare mighty things, to win glorious triumphs, even though checkered by failure, than to take rank with those poor spirits who neither enjoy much nor suffer much, because they live in the gray twilight that knows not victory nor defeat.

T Roosevelt

104

PRESCRIPTION

Although seldom sensational, small efforts are essential. With grooming, small stones and grains of sand make a road. With repeated single strokes the artist reveals a masterpiece. And so it is with God's hand, who stretches his fingers over our lifespan, taking our tiny efforts and weaving a life of meaning, purpose, and contentment.

JA Lacy

PRESCRIPTION

For we are God's workmanship, created in Christ Jesus to do good works, which God prepared in advance for us to do.

Ephesians 2:10

106

PRESCRIPTION

A man without ambition is dead. A man with ambition but no love is dead. A man with ambition and love for his blessings here on earth is ever so alive. Having been alive, it won't be so hard in the end to lie down and rest.

P Bailey

PRESCRIPTION

But now, this is what the LORD says:
"Fear not, for I have redeemed you; I have
summoned you by name; you are mine."

Isaiah 43:1

PRESCRIPTION

The secret of my success? It is simple.
It is found in the Bible, "In all thy ways
acknowledge Him and He shall direct
thy paths." (Proverbs 3:6)

GW Carver

PRESCRIPTION

He who would introduce into public affairs
the principles of Christianity will change
the face of the world.

B Franklin

110

PRESCRIPTION

Do you not know that your body is a temple
of the Holy Spirit, who is in you, whom you have
received from God? You are not your own; you
were bought at a price. Therefore honor God
with your body.

1 Corinthians 6:19-20

PRESCRIPTION

Lord, give me love and strength and
compassion to help all I meet, especially those
less fortunate than I. Insofar as possible, let
me be a working and living substance reflecting
the purity of Your love.

JA Lacy

PRESCRIPTION

If there is righteousness in the heart, there will be beauty in the character, and harmony in the home. If there is harmony in the home, there will be order in the nation. If there is order in the nation, there will be peace in the world.

Author unknown

PRESCRIPTION

Taste and see that the LORD is good; blessed
is the man who takes refuge in him.

Psalm 34:8

PRESCRIPTION

How do you make a day holy?
By seeing that it is holy already; and
behaving accordingly.

JD Lewis

PRESCRIPTION

Love your neighbor as yourself.

Romans 13:9

PRESCRIPTION

Where there is charity and wisdom,
  there is neither fear nor ignorance.
Where there is patience and humility,
  there is neither anger nor vexation.
Where there is poverty and joy,
  there is neither greed nor avarice.
Where there is peace and meditation,
  there is neither anxiety nor doubt.

St. Francis of Assisi

PRESCRIPTION

Your lifestyle habits can affect your lifespan.

Moderation. Moderation is a common denominator in all phases of life, including diet, work, and physical activity.

Outlook. Keep a positive one.

Relationships. Maintain your friendships and the love of your family.

JA Lacy and R Lacy

PRESCRIPTION

Be kind and compassionate
to one another, forgiving each other,
just as in Christ God forgave you.

Ephesians 4:32

119

PRESCRIPTION

To laugh often and much; to win the respect
of intelligent people and affection of children;
to earn the appreciation of honest critics and
endure the betrayal of false friends; to appreciate
beauty, to find the best in others; to leave the
world a bit better, to know even one life has
breathed easier because you have lived.
This is to have succeeded.

T Roosevelt

℞ PRESCRIPTION

All men dream: but not equally. Those who dream by night in the dusty recesses of their minds wake in the day to find that it was vanity: but the dreamers of the day are dangerous men, for they may act on their dream with open eyes, to make it possible.

TE Lawrence

PRESCRIPTION

And now these three remain: faith, hope and love. But the greatest of these is love.

1 Corinthians 13:13

PRESCRIPTION

Three things guarantee a hopeful future:
God's blessing, efficient planning,
and labor.

JA Lacy

PRESCRIPTION

There is a time for everything, and a season for every activity under heaven: a time to be born and a time to die, a time to plant and a time to uproot, a time to weep and a time to laugh, a time to mourn and a time to dance, a time to keep and a time to throw away, a time to be silent and a time to speak, a time to love and a time to hate, a time for war and a time for peace.

Ecclesiastes 3:1-8

PRESCRIPTION

Every man has a train of thought on which he rides when he is alone. The dignity and nobility of his life, as well as his happiness, depends upon the direction in which that train is going, the baggage it carries, and the scenery through which it travels.

Author unknown

PRESCRIPTION

Do not be anxious about anything, but in everything, by prayer and petition, with thanksgiving, present your requests to God. And the peace of God, which transcends all understanding, will guard your hearts and your minds in Christ Jesus.

Philippians 4:6,7

PRESCRIPTION

Research by Doctor Randy Byrd of San Francisco General Hospital has shown a statistical difference in recovery rates of heart patients who were prayed for over those who were not. Also, studies show that people who believe in God generally have lower blood pressure and are healthier than nonbelievers.

PRESCRIPTION

The LORD gives life to everything.

Nehemiah 9:6

128

PRESCRIPTION

I hold not with the pessimist that all things are ill, nor with the optimist that all things are well. All things are not well, but all things shall be well, because this is God's world.

Browning

PRESCRIPTION

Love the LORD your God with all
your heart and with all your soul and
with all your strength.

Deuteronomy 6:5

PRESCRIPTION

The capacity to believe is the most significant and fundamental human faculty, and the most important thing about a man is what he believes in the depth of his being. That is the thing that makes him what he is; the thing that organizes him and feeds him; the thing that keeps him going in the face of untoward circumstances; the thing that gives him resistance and drive. Let neutrality, confusion, indifference, or skepticism enter this inner place, and the very springs of life will cease to flow.

HS Tigner

PRESCRIPTION

Wisdom is better than strength.

Ecclesiastes 9:16

PRESCRIPTION

Faith embodies an inner conviction
of the supremacy of God.

Author Unknown

PRESCRIPTION

He who pursues righteousness and love finds life, prosperity and honor.

Proverbs 21:21

PRESCRIPTION

What will today bring?

God has given me this day to use as I will. I can waste it or use it for good. What I do today is important, because I'm exchanging a day of my life for it. When tomorrow comes this day will be gone forever, leaving in its place something I have traded for it. I want it to be gain, not loss; good, not evil; success, not failure. In order that I shall not regret the price I paid for it.

The Sports Medicine Foundation of America, Inc.

135

PRESCRIPTION

Beginning the day with God and
keeping a positive attitude help foster
an abundant life.

JA Lacy

PRESCRIPTION

This is the day the LORD has made;
let us rejoice and be glad in it.

Psalm 118:24

PRESCRIPTION

Be thoughtful of others' opinions. There are three sides to every controversy—yours, the others'—and the right one.

Author Unknown

PRESCRIPTION

A cheerful heart is good medicine, but a crushed spirit dries up the bones.

Proverbs 17:22

PRESCRIPTION

He who has heart has hope, and he who has hope has everything.

Middle Eastern Proverb

PRESCRIPTION

There is only one permanent way to have the peace of soul that wells up in joy, contentment and happiness, and that is by repentance of sin and by personal faith in Jesus Christ as Savior.

B Graham

PRESCRIPTION

God changes times and seasons; he sets up kings and deposes them. He gives wisdom to the wise and knowledge to the discerning.

Daniel 2:21

PRESCRIPTION

I am convinced that life is 10% of what happens to me and 90% how I react to it.

C Swindoll

PRESCRIPTION

To seek God, is the greatest adventure. To find Him, the greatest human achievement.

R Simon

PRESCRIPTION

God sends his love and his faithfulness.

Psalm 57:3

145

PRESCRIPTION

In God's will is our peace.

D Alighieri

PRESCRIPTION

A wise man once said that God is only a prayer away. One of the most powerful blessings God has given his people is access to him. Psalm 17 says: "I call on you, O God, for you will answer me." Prayer is more than a monologue; it's a dialogue.

JA Lacy

PRESCRIPTION

The LORD is slow to anger, abounding in
love and forgiving sin and rebellion.

Numbers 14:18

PRESCRIPTION

God is only a prayer away.

C Swindoll

PRESCRIPTION

The greatest essentials of happiness are something to do, something to love, and something to hope for.

Author Unknown

PRESCRIPTION

An anxious heart weighs a man down, but a kind word cheers him up.

Proverbs 12:25

PRESCRIPTION

Contentment comes when I have faith
in God and let him do the "worrying"
about my life.

S Sheppard

PRESCRIPTION

Greater love has no one than this, that he
lay down his life for his friends.

John 15:13

PRESCRIPTION

Cherish all your happy moments; they
make a fine cushion for old age.

C Morley

PRESCRIPTION

Teach me your way, O LORD, and I will walk
in your truth; give me an undivided heart,
that I may fear your name.

Psalm 86:11

PRESCRIPTION

When you have read the Bible, you will know
that it is the Word of God because you will have
found in it the key to your own heart, your own
happiness, and your own duty.

W Wilson

PRESCRIPTION

Getting anything we want is not the secret
to success or happiness. It's having God's
grace to enjoy what we have.

JA Lacy

PRESCRIPTION

Who is wise and understanding among you? Let him show it by his good life, by deeds done in the humility that comes from wisdom.

James 3:13

PRESCRIPTION

Be generous with praise,
cautious with criticism.

Author Unknown

PRESCRIPTION

For with God is the fountain of life;
in his light we see light.

Psalm 36:9